A PRIMER
ON
COMMERCIAL
REAL ESTATE

Building the Foundation for Success

WILLIAM H. HOLLY

This book is dedicated to my wife Allison who has faithfully stood by my side on the rising tides and the rocky shoals of a career in commercial real estate. Thank you for joining me on this lifelong voyage together.

Table of Contents

Chapter One: Setting the Foundation—Understanding Commercial Real Estate 7
- Defining Commercial Real Estate
- Key Players in the Industry
- The Benefits and Risks of Commercial Real Estate
- Essential Skills for Success

Chapter Two: Your First Investment Deal—Practical Steps to Get Started 19
- Assessing Your Financial Situation
- Understanding Key Investment Metrics
- Finding Your Niche and Evaluating Properties
- Financing Your First Deal: Options and Strategies

Chapter Three: Effective Property Management—Creating Value and Efficiency 27
- The Role of Property Management
- Maximizing Property Performance
- Enhancing Value Through Strategic Improvements
- Technology and Automation in Property Management

Chapter 4: Breaking into Brokerage—Building a Commercial Real Estate Career 35
- The Role of a Commercial Real Estate Broker
- Key Skills for a Successful Brokerage Career
- Building Your Personal Brand
- Starting Your Own Firm vs. Joining a Brokerage

Chapter 5: Cutting-Edge Marketing—Outproducing Your Competition with Modern Strategies 45

- Leveraging Social Media: TikTok, Reels, and More
- AI in Real Estate Marketing
- Content Strategies for Building Authority
- Video Podcasts and Long-Form Content

Chapter 6: Common Pitfalls in Commercial Real Estate—and How to Avoid Them 55

- Mistakes New Investors Make
- Risks in Property Management
- Avoiding Common Brokerage Missteps
- How to Build Resilience and Learn from Setbacks

Chapter 7: Leveraging Relationships —Networking and Partnerships in Real Estate... 65

- The Power of Relationships in Real Estate
- Strategic Partnerships and Collaboration
- Building a Real Estate Network
- Case Studies of Successful Partnerships

Chapter 8: Long-Term Success in Commercial Real Estate 75

- Reinvesting Profits for Growth
- Managing Market Cycles
- Planning for Succession and Legacy
- Sustaining Growth in Changing Markets

Chapter 9: Leadership and Mindset —The Qualities of a Successful Investor.. 85

- Developing a Leadership Mindset
- Embracing Resilience in the Face of Challenges

- Maintaining a Positive Attitude and Adaptability
- Leading by Example and Building Trust

Chapter 10: The Future of Commercial Real Estate—Embracing Innovation and New Opportunities...95
- The Rise of Smart Building Technologies
- The Importance of Sustainability and Green Building Practices
- Adapting to Flexible Work Arrangements
- Leveraging Data Analytics and Mixed-Use Developments

CHAPTER ONE

Setting the Foundation— Understanding Commercial Real Estate

When I first entered the commercial real estate business, I was immediately captivated by its complexity, its potential for transformation, and the critical role it played in shaping cities and building communities. It was more than a profession—it was a living, breathing force that had the power to shape entire communities, influence economies, and create wealth for those who truly understood how to navigate it. Commercial real estate is more than just about buildings or properties—it's about the intersection of commerce, people, and spaces. It encompasses the history of a place and its people. It incorporates how those spaces affect the lives of those who use them and the economic ecosystems that develop around them. More than that, it's about seeing opportunity where others see only concrete and steel.

I can still remember walking through the bustling streets of downtown Miami in my early years, looking up at the towering skyscrapers and realizing that these were not just structures—they were the backbones of the economy. These buildings housed offices, retail stores, and residential units, creating a space where people worked, shopped, and lived their lives. Each building had its own story, purpose, and role in the grand scheme of things. I knew from that moment that commercial real estate was the space I wanted to make my mark.

For those unfamiliar with the term, commercial real estate, it refers to any property that is used for business purposes. It's a broad field that include office buildings, retail centers, industrial warehouses, and multifamily apartment buildings, all with the aim of generating income. It's an industry that requires a blend of vision, strategy, teamwork and practical execution.

I've often found myself explaining to others that the business proposition for commercial real estate lies in its ability to generate income through these various types of property. However, whether it's a towering office building in the middle of a bustling city or a quiet suburban retail center, commercial real estate exists to create value—not just for its owners, but for the community. I quickly learned that the scope of this industry was massive. By 2022, the global commercial real estate market was valued at over $3.4 trillion, underscoring its significance not just as a driver of economic activity, but as a critical part of the world economy. It's an industry that touches every aspect of society, from where we work and shop to where we live and socialize.

But what makes commercial real estate so unique and different from other forms of investment? The answer lies in its ability to generate recurring revenue, appreciation over time, and provision of both short-term and long-term financial gains. A single office building can house dozens of companies, each paying rent which contribute to the building's revenue stream, and in turn, the economy around it. A well-placed retail center can become a hub for local businesses, drawing in customers and stimulating local economies. The possibilities are endless, but they all begin with understanding the core principles of the industry and the risks associated with debt used in almost all commercial real estate transactions

A Personal Journey into Commercial Real Estate

When I first stepped into this world, I was green—eager but unsure. Like most of my young peers, I had not studied commercial real estate in college. My first real project was not a high-rise building in a big city or a glamorous shopping mall; it was a small office complex in an area of Miami that had seen better days. At first glance, it didn't look like much, but that's the thing about commercial real estate—success isn't just about what's in front of you; it's about seeing what could be.

The office complex had been neglected for years. The exterior was faded, the interior spaces were outdated, and the tenants were barely scraping by. But I saw the potential. The location was good—just a few miles from a thriving business district—and the building itself had solid bones. It just needed someone to invest the time and effort to bring it back to life. I envisioned the offices being rejuvenated with new paint and carpet as well as welcoming new tenants who were new start-up businesses. I visualized the parking lot full, and the surrounding businesses benefiting from this increased foot traffic.

The first challenge I faced was securing financing. Commercial real estate deals often require significant upfront capital, and as a young developer without a lengthy track record, convincing lenders to back my vision was no easy task. Communication is key in Commercial real estate. I spent a lot of time preparing investment offerings and loan packages for banks. Most banks would not give me a chance, but I viewed every loan officer as a person whom I needed to clearly paint a vision of what could be and not what it currently was. However, all the bankers would go straight to the numbers and so I refined and tweaked my business plans many times with the lessons learned from my failed attempts. Finally, after months of getting NO's from every banker, I finally got one YES…and that's all you need. Persistence had paid off. The lesson I learned in those early days was that vision alone isn't enough; you need to back it up with a concrete financial plan that others can not only believe in but can get approved by a loan committee consisting of seasoned veterans who have seen every way a deal can fail.

Once financing was in place, the next challenge was managing the renovation process. In commercial real estate, one of the keys to success is creating value, and often that means taking a property that is underperforming or outdated and giving it a new lease on life. For the office complex, this meant everything from updating the heating, ventilation and air conditioning (HVAC) system, which would allow the Landlord (me) to charge for electricity separate from the rent, to painting the interior of the office spaces (yes, Myself!), thereby improving the landscaping and making a good first impression when tenants and visitors visit the building. It was a long and often frustrating process, but it was also one of the most rewarding experiences of my career. Every improvement we made brought us one step closer to realizing the vision I had for the building.

But perhaps the most critical aspect of this project was securing tenants. A commercial building is only as valuable as its ability to generate income, and that income comes from tenants who are willing to pay for the space. In the case of this office complex, attracting new tenants was a challenge. The building's reputation had suffered over the years, and many potential tenants were hesitant to move into a space that had been neglected for so long. This is where the importance of relationships in commercial real estate became clear to me. By leveraging my network and building trust with local businesses, I was able to slowly fill the offices with new tenants. It wasn't an overnight success, but by focusing on providing value—competitive rental rates, modern amenities, and a commitment to maintaining the property—I was able to turn the complex into a thriving business hub.

Looking back, that first project taught me lessons that have guided me throughout my career. I learned that success in commercial real estate is about more than just the physical building itself—it's about understanding the needs of the market, being able to see opportunities where others see obstacles, and having the perseverance to follow through on your vision.

Understanding the Players in Commercial Real Estate

As I grew in the business, I came to understand that commercial real estate is a highly collaborative industry. It's a field where relationships are paramount, and success often depends on your ability to work with a wide range of professionals. Every project I've worked on involved a team of experts, each playing a crucial role in the success of the development.

I learned early on the value of working closely with brokers, property managers, and contractors. For instance, brokers are often the bridge between property owners and potential tenants or buyers. A good broker can help you navigate the complexities of the market, identify opportunities, and secure deals that may not have been on your radar,. Property managers, on the other hand, are essential for the long-term success of any development. They handle the day-to-day operations, build out the tenant spaces, ensure that tenants are happy, and maintain the property and control costs so that the project continues to generate income.

In one of my larger projects—a mixed-use development that combined retail, office, and residential spaces—the importance of these relationships became even clearer. The success of that project wasn't just about securing financing or overseeing construction; it was about working closely with a diverse team of experts to ensure that every aspect of the development, and ultimately its operations with competing interests, from different types of tenants, ran smoothly. The property manager played a critical role in maintaining the building's value over time and keeping the tenants happy, while the broker helped secure high-quality tenants that kept occupancy rates high and rents stable.

The Benefits and Risks of Commercial Real Estate

As with any investment, commercial real estate carries its share of risks and rewards. When I talk with new investors, one of the first things I tell them is that commercial real estate is not a get-rich-quick scheme. Commercial Real Estate is a get rich slow process. It requires patience, diligence, and a deep understanding of the market. The potential for significant financial rewards is there, but so is the risk of loss.

The biggest dangers are usually from people. It is paramount that systems are put in place and checks and balances to counter any of people's lesser angels. A property manager stealing money can end a company and bankrupt a project.

The top three risks that most businesses do not consider are: dishonest employees, litigation risk and debt risk which includes rising interest rates or a banking crisis. All three have toppled excellent firms with good people.

Systems and Checks and balances will allow you to minimize these risks, but they are never eliminated. I've found that the best avenue to avoid these risks, or to survive them if they are unavoidable, is to include professionals on your team such as a certified public accountant (CPA), a very good attorney and/or a more experienced senior partner. I cannot emphasize the importance of surrounding yourself with the best qualified, experienced and ethical professionals to bolster your internal team.

One of the key benefits of commercial real estate is its potential for generating stable, recurring income. Unlike residential leases, which typically last one-year, commercial leases often span several years, providing a steady stream of income for property owners. In some of my projects, leases have extended for 10 years or more, offering long-term financial stability. This is particularly true in office buildings or retail centers, where landlords and tenants may invest heavily in customizing their spaces and are therefore more likely to commit to longer leases.

However, this stability comes with its own set of challenges. Finding the right tenants is critical, as vacancies can significantly impact a property's profitability. When a tenant vacates a commercial property, it often takes a longer time to find a replacement compared to residential properties. Also, vacant spaces require further investment in construction, called tenant improvements, which further increases the capital needed to maintain cash flow. This is something I've experienced firsthand, particularly during economic downturns when businesses are hesitant to commit to new leases. For example, during the financial crisis of 2008, many of my properties lost several tenants as their businesses struggled to survive. It was a difficult time, but by staying proactive—offering temporary rent reductions and improving the property's amenities—I was able to retain other tenants and eventually attract new ones once the economy stabilized. The two most important things to do in a crisis are to clearly communicate with your tenants and to keep your lender fully informed. Remember, the smartest real estate people don't survive downturns, it is the best capitalized and those with the best banking relationships who survive. Believe me, I learned that lesson the hard way when all my banks went out of business in 2008. Lesson learned.

Another important factor to consider is property appreciation. Over time, well-located and well-maintained commercial properties tend to increase in value. I've seen properties in prime locations double in value over the course of a decade. However, property appreciation is not guaranteed, and it's heavily influenced by external factors such as market conditions, local economic trends, and even changes in government policy. Typically, commercial real estate is a good hedge against inflation as appreciation usually keeps up with or outperforms inflation. In one instance, I acquired a property in an up-and-coming neighborhood, expecting its value to rise as new developments moved into the area. While the neighborhood did improve, a sudden change in zoning regulations limited the potential for new construction, which slowed the pace of growth. The lesson learned here was that while property appreciation can be a significant driver of wealth in commercial real estate, it's essential to stay informed about local policies and market trends that could impact your investment. Governmental zoning and Fed policy are two important areas to be mindful of as the commercial real estate investor does not have control over them and they affect properties greatly.

Building Your Knowledge Base and Setting Your Foundation

As I've shared throughout this chapter, understanding commercial real estate is much more than just about acquiring properties. It's about grasping the fundamentals—market dynamics, governmental policies, the banking and debt markets, risk mitigation, relationship management, and value creation. Over the years, I've learned that the most successful investors and developers are those who take the time to truly understand the markets, implement systems in their businesses and mitigate their risk regarding personnel, litigation, debt and market factors. This industry is filled with opportunities, but only for those who are willing to put in the work and weather the inevitable storms which will come.

When I speak to newcomers in the industry, I often tell them that the first step is education. You need to learn the language of commercial real estate—the terms, the metrics, and the strategies that drive success. You need to understand the different property types, how to assess market conditions, and how to evaluate a property's potential for generating income. But beyond that, you need to cultivate relationships, because commercial real estate is ultimately a people business. The deals I've closed and the projects I've developed wouldn't have been possible without the relationships and partnerships I've built along the way.

CHAPTER TWO

Your First Investment Deal—Practical Steps to Get Started

When I reflect on the first commercial property deal, I ever closed, it's impossible not to remember the mixture of excitement and anxiety that came with it. I was young, eager, and had a strong vision for what I wanted to accomplish, but I was also aware of the risks I was taking. In many ways, commercial real estate can be daunting for first-time investors. The stakes feel higher, the numbers are bigger, and the complexities are much greater compared to residential real estate. But as I've learned over the years, the more deals under your belt, the path ahead becomes clearer.

My first commercial property deal wasn't in a flashy high-rise or a sought-after urban center. It was a modest office building in a part of Miami that was underdeveloped at the time. The property wasn't in perfect shape, but I saw potential where others didn't. I realized that success in commercial real estate doesn't always come from finding the perfect property—sometimes, it comes from seeing what a property *could* be.

That first deal was the gateway into a career I'm still passionate about today, and the lessons I learned then are ones I carry with me on every new investment. In this chapter, I'll walk you through the steps you need to take to land your first commercial real estate deal, including assessing your financial situation, evaluating properties, and understanding financing options. The road to your first deal may be challenging, but with the right mindset and preparation, it can be incredibly rewarding.

Assessing Your Financial Situation

Before you even think about signing a contract or touring properties, the first step is to take a hard look at your financial situation. In commercial real estate, having a clear understanding of your finances is crucial. This is something I had to learn very quickly when I first started out. Commercial real estate investments often require more upfront capital than residential properties, and as a new investor, you need to know exactly how much capital you need not only for the acquisition but also for reserves (which many neglect to their peril) and for operating expenses until you can get the property stabilized. It's very important that your deals are conservatively underwritten. During the financing period it is better to be conservative than to be optimistic (that can come later when you are marketing the project).

When I was preparing for my first deal, I spent weeks reviewing my financial projections. I created detailed budgets that included estimates for everything—down payments, closing costs, renovations, reserves and operational expenses. I wanted to make sure I had a clear picture of what I was getting into. Without understanding your cash flow, it's nearly impossible to make informed decisions about the types of properties you can afford to purchase.

Commercial real estate investments require a strong handle on certain financial metrics. For instance, you need to be familiar with terms like Net Operating Income (NOI), which represents a property's income after all operating expenses have been subtracted. In my first deal, calculating the NOI allowed me to understand what kind of returns I could expect after covering operating costs like property taxes, insurance, professional fees and maintenance.

Financing is often the trickiest part of the process for first-time investors. When I was just starting, I didn't have a long track record to show lenders, so I had to be especially meticulous in my financial planning. Many lenders look for a clear demonstration of the property's earning potential before approving a loan. This means understanding how much revenue the property can generate and whether that income can cover the debt service (your loan payments) with a cushion for unexpected market changes. It's essential to know your Debt Service Coverage Ratio (DSCR), which is a metric that measures the property's ability to cover its loan payments. Lenders generally want to see a DSCR of at least 1.25, meaning the property's income should be 25% higher than the debt service. In softer markets, that number can increase to 1.3 or 1.35 for more speculative projects.

Finding the Right Property: Seeing Potential Where Others Don't

When I was searching for my first commercial property, I quickly realized that the best deals weren't necessarily in prime locations or high-end buildings. Instead, they were in places where others saw challenges, but I saw opportunity. In my case, that meant purchasing an underperforming office building in a less desirable area of Miami. It was a risk, no doubt, but I believed in the area's potential for growth and knew that if I could improve the building and attract the right tenants, I could turn it into a profitable investment.

One of the most important aspects of finding the right property is understanding the market you're entering. In my case, Miami's office market was beginning to evolve, and there was an increasing demand for affordable office spaces that didn't sacrifice quality. That's where my opportunity lay. I knew that by offering competitive pricing, improving the building's appearance, having ready to go office suites and improving the amenities, I could fill a niche in the market.

Market analysis plays a huge role in evaluating properties. I believe you make money when you buy. The better the price goes in, the better your performance will be. Before committing to any property, you need to thoroughly research the local market, its trends, and the demand for the type of property you're considering. For me, understanding Miami's business environment and recognizing the areas poised for growth was critical in making my first deal a success. In fact, much of my decision-making was informed by trends and data, such as Miami's growing demand for small to mid-sized office spaces, which I gathered from market reports published by reputable sources.

Financing Your First Deal: Options and Strategies

Securing financing for your first commercial property can be one of the most daunting parts of the process. When I was starting out, I knew that I needed to explore all my financing options if I wanted to close the deal. Commercial real estate typically requires more capital upfront than residential properties, which can be intimidating for new investors. However, with the right preparation and a strong business plan, it's possible to secure financing that works for you.

In my case, I approached several traditional lenders, including local banks and credit unions. I also explored alternative financing options, such as working with private investors who were willing to provide capital in exchange for a share of the profits. What I learned during this process is that lenders want to see more than just a property—they want to see a plan. I had to present detailed financial projections, including anticipated cash flow, potential risks, and a timeline for improvements.

Financing methods in commercial real estate vary, and it's important to explore which option works best for your specific deal. Some of the most common financing options include traditional loans from banks, Small Business Administration (SBA) loans, and bridge loans, which are short-term loans often used to finance a property while longer-term financing is arranged. However, be very careful with bridge loans as they carry much higher interest rates. You can also consider working with private equity firms or real estate investment trusts (REITs) if the deal is large enough, later in your career

For my first deal, I used a combination of a traditional bank loan and a private investor who helped me cover the renovation costs in exchange for a percentage of the profits. This hybrid approach allowed me to mitigate some of the risks while ensuring I had the capital needed to move forward with the project.

Another important lesson I learned early on was the importance of having a contingency often called a reserve fund. Commercial real estate deals are often complex, and unexpected costs can arise at any time. During the renovation of my first property, we discovered that the building needed more extensive repairs than originally anticipated. This increased the overall cost of the project, but because I had set aside a contingency fund, I was able to cover these expenses without derailing the project.

Closing the Deal and Moving Forward

After months of preparation, negotiations, and securing financing, I was finally ready to close on my first commercial property. The day we closed the deal was one of the most exhilarating moments of my career. It felt like the culmination of all my hard work and planning. But as any seasoned real estate investor will tell you, closing the deal is just the beginning. The real work begins once you take ownership of the property.

Once the deal was closed, I immediately set to work on improving the property. We upgraded the common areas, modernized the building's systems, and enhanced the exterior to attract new tenants. It wasn't easy—there were days when I wondered if I'd taken on more than I could handle and I spent many sleepless nights worried about making sure we had enough money to cover the debt service for the bank loan—but step by step, the property transformed into a thriving office complex.

One of the key lessons I learned during this process was the importance of patience. Commercial real estate is not a quick-win industry. It takes time to see the results of your efforts, but if you stay focused and stick to your plan, the rewards can be significant. That first property eventually became the foundation of my real estate portfolio, and it taught me invaluable lessons about managing risk, creating value, and building long-term wealth.

Conclusion: The Beginning of Your Real Estate Journey

Closing your first commercial real estate deal is a major milestone, but it's just the beginning of a much larger journey. The lessons you learn from that first deal—about finances, property evaluation, tenant management, and value creation—will serve as the foundation for every future investment you make. I've found that the first deal is often the hardest, but it's also the most important. Once you've taken that leap, you'll gain the confidence and experience needed to tackle even more ambitious projects but remember, the bigger the project the bigger the challenge. Fortunately, along the way, you will build your commercial real estate muscles to be able to handle bigger challenges and benefit from bigger opportunities

My journey in commercial real estate began with that modest office building, but it set the stage for everything that came after. The process of securing financing, evaluating properties, and managing tenants may seem overwhelming at first, but with hard work, persistence and a clear vision, you'll find your footing. And as you continue to grow and evolve as an investor, each deal will bring new opportunities and new lessons.

Remember, the key to success in commercial real estate is not just about the properties themselves—it's about the people, the execution of your plan, and to re-envisioning of what is today and what can be in the future. Your first deal is just the start. The possibilities ahead are endless.

CHAPTER THREE:

Effective Property Management—Creating Value and Efficiency

When I first started investing in commercial real estate, I quickly learned that buying a property is only half the battle. The other half—and often the more critical aspect—is property management and proper daily execution of running buildings, budgets and construction projects. I realized early on that an investment property's long-term success and profitability depended heavily on how well it was managed. Solid execution in property management can transform a modest asset into a thriving, income-generating investment. On the flip side, poor management can turn even the best property into a financial burden.

In my early days as an investor, I managed my properties myself. I thought, "How hard can it be?" But soon enough, I was overwhelmed by tenant issues, maintenance calls, and the sheer volume of daily tasks that came with keeping a property running smoothly. It didn't take long for me to realize that property management was not something I could handle casually. It required dedicated focus, and more importantly, there was no substitute for the daily hard work of property management. There is no shortcut to good property management, it takes a fully committed team that is available at any time for any emergency. We have had building fires, floods and hurricanes and property managers are the first responders of commercial real estate.

In this chapter, I'll dive into the importance of property management and the strategies you can use to maximize a property's value. Whether you're managing your own property or working with a professional property management team, the principles remain the same: you need to keep tenants happy, control costs, minimize risk and continuously seek opportunities to add value.

The Role of Property Management in Commercial Real Estate

Effective property management is all about maintaining and improving a property to ensure that the property runs efficiently within budget while remaining attractive to tenants and continues to generate revenue. This involves everything from handling tenant relations and maintenance requests to overseeing repairs, budgeting, and sometimes leasing. A well-managed property not only attracts higher-quality tenants but also retains them for longer periods, minimizing vacancy rates and ensuring a steady income stream. In my opinion, this is a key element to financial success in commercial real estate. It is always cheaper to keep a tenant, even at a discount, than to have downtime with vacancy, marketing and leasing costs, and new construction of improvements to secure a new tenant.

In my early years of property ownership, I had a small office complex that required a lot of attention. The tenants were primarily small businesses, and while they didn't need much space, they expected a certain level of service and attention. I quickly learned that responsive, proactive management with constant communication was key to keeping these tenants happy and renewing their leases year after year. I made it a point to address maintenance issues quickly, keep common areas clean and well-lit, and ensure that rent collection was handled efficiently. These small efforts had a big impact on tenant satisfaction, and over time, I noticed that my vacancy rates stayed low, and my tenant turnover was minimal.

Research has shown that tenant satisfaction is directly linked to property performance. Studies from the National Association of Real Estate Investment Trusts (NAREIT) have found that properties with higher tenant satisfaction typically have lower vacancy rates and higher net operating income (NOI). This aligns with my personal experience: when tenants feel that their needs are being met, they're more likely to renew their leases, which means a more consistent income and fewer vacancies to fill.

Maximizing Property Performance: The Importance of Maintenance and Operations

One of the most critical aspects of property management is ensuring that the building operates efficiently. This includes everything from routine maintenance to major repairs, and it's an area that can significantly impact a property's profitability if not handled properly. In my experience, regular, proactive maintenance is one of the best ways to keep operating costs under control. It's much cheaper to fix a minor issue before it becomes a major problem. For example, a small leak in the roof might only cost a few hundred dollars to repair, but if left unchecked, it could lead to water damage and thousands of dollars in repairs.

When I took over one of my first office buildings, I made it a point to conduct regular inspections of the property. I walked through the building with my maintenance team, checked the condition of the HVAC systems, plumbing, and electrical systems, and noted any areas that needed attention. By staying ahead of potential problems, I was able to avoid costly repairs and keep the property running smoothly.

One of the most effective ways to improve property performance is through technology. Over the past decade, advances in property management software and automation tools have made it easier than ever to track maintenance requests, manage budgets, and communicate with tenants. For example, many modern property management platforms allow tenants to submit maintenance requests online, which can be tracked and addressed in real-time. These systems also provide valuable data on tenant behavior and property performance, allowing you to make more informed decisions about where to allocate resources and how to improve operations.

In addition to day-to-day operations, it's important to have a plan in place for capital improvements—larger, long-term investments that enhance the property's value. These can include anything from upgrading the HVAC system to renovating common areas or adding new amenities. In my experience, well-timed capital improvements can significantly boost a property's value and make it more attractive to potential tenants. I've seen this firsthand with one of my retail properties, where a renovation of the common areas, new paint on the façade and re-striping the parking lot not only attracted higher-end tenants but also allowed me to raise rents.

Enhancing Tenant Relations and Retention Strategies

Keeping tenants satisfied is perhaps the most important aspect of property management. In commercial real estate, tenant turnover can be costly, not just in terms of lost rent but also in terms of the expenses involved in marketing the space, renovating it for new tenants, and negotiating new leases. In fact, research shows that it can cost significantly more to attract a new tenant than to retain an existing one. This is why tenant retention is a top priority for any successful property management strategy.

Over the years, I've found that building strong relationships with tenants is key to keeping them happy and ensuring they stay long-term. This doesn't mean just responding to their requests when something breaks—it means anticipating their needs, maintaining open lines of communication, and creating a sense of community within the property.

In one of my office properties, I noticed that tenants valued small perks, like well-maintained common areas, fast internet service, and accessible parking. While these might seem like minor details, they made a big difference in how tenants felt about the space. I also made an effort to meet with tenants regularly, check in on their needs, and address any concerns they had. This proactive approach helped me create a positive relationship with tenants, which ultimately led to higher retention rates and fewer vacancies. Moreover, we typically have several tenants' events per year, including lunches or desserts, in the lobby of buildings or special baskets and treats around the holidays delivered to the tenants' offices.

Another important aspect of tenant retention is flexibility. In today's rapidly changing business environment, many commercial tenants are looking for more flexible lease terms, shorter lease periods, or even co-working options. I've adapted to this trend by offering flexible leasing options on some of my properties, which has helped me attract and retain tenants who might otherwise have chosen a different space. Being willing to negotiate lease terms that meet the specific needs of tenants has been one of the most effective strategies I've used for tenant retention.

Creating Value Through Strategic Improvements

One of the key principles I've followed throughout my career is that property management should always focus on *adding value*. This means continuously looking for ways to enhance the property, whether through renovations, improved tenant services, or operational efficiencies. In commercial real estate, adding value isn't just about aesthetics—it's about creating a better experience for tenants while increasing the property's financial performance.

For example, I once acquired an older office building that had a high vacancy rate and a reputation for being outdated. The first thing I did was invest in strategic improvements. I upgraded the lobby and common areas, added energy-efficient lighting, and installed a modern HVAC system. These improvements not only made the building more attractive to potential tenants but also reduced the building's operating costs by improving energy efficiency. As a result, I was able to fill the vacant spaces and raise rents, which significantly increased the property's value.

Sustainability is another area where property improvements can add value. In recent years, there has been a growing demand for environmentally friendly buildings, and I've found that incorporating green building practices can be a smart investment. When I developed Miami Green, the first Leadership in Energy and Environmental Design (LEED) certified office building in Miami, I knew that sustainability was more than just a buzzword—it was a trend that was here to stay. The building's energy-efficient design not only reduced operating costs but also attracted environmentally conscious tenants who were willing to pay a premium for space in a green building.

Studies show that properties with sustainable features, such as energy-efficient systems, renewable energy sources, and green certifications like LEED, tend to have lower operating costs and higher tenant satisfaction. These features can also make a property more attractive to institutional investors, who are increasingly prioritizing sustainability in their portfolios.

Conclusion: The Art of Property Management

Property management is both an art and a science. It's about balancing the day-to-day operations with the long-term strategy of adding value and ensuring the property remains a profitable investment. Over the years, I've come to appreciate that effective property management is not just about keeping tenants happy or maintaining the building—it's about creating a space where businesses can thrive and people chose to be, while working to ensure that expenses at the property are competitive. Tenants appreciate when the property management team runs a building on budget and efficiently as the tenants realize it is their rent which pays the bills.

Managing a commercial property requires careful attention to detail, daily effort, proactive forecasting, and a focus on delivering value to both tenants and investors. Whether you're managing a small office building or a large retail center, the principles remain the same: treat your tenants with respect, keep the property in top condition, and always be on the lookout for opportunities to enhance value and to economize on operating expenses. In my experience, these strategies will not only help you maximize the property's performance but also set you up for long-term success in the competitive world of commercial real estate.

CHAPTER 4

Breaking into Brokerage—Building a Commercial Real Estate Career

When I first started in commercial real estate, I had little understanding of what it truly meant to be a broker. Like many, I thought the job was mostly about showing properties and negotiating deals. It wasn't long before I realized that successful brokerage required much more than that. It's embodies building relationships, understanding market dynamics, understanding the business needs and trends of companies seeking commercial space and positioning yourself as an expert in your niche. The journey from being a newcomer in the industry to becoming a recognized broker with a reputation for closing major deals is one filled with learning, persistence, and the ability to adapt.

As I reflect on my early days, it's clear to me that there's no single path to becoming a successful commercial real estate broker. Everyone's journey is unique and shaped by their background, skills, and experiences. However, there are common lessons and principles that can guide anyone who's looking to break into the brokerage side of commercial real estate and build a rewarding career.

Understanding the Role of a Commercial Real Estate Broker

Before diving into the specific strategies and steps, it's essential to understand what a commercial real estate broker does. Unlike residential agents, commercial brokers deal with properties that generate income—office buildings, retail spaces, industrial facilities, and multifamily properties. These transactions are typically more complex, involving detailed financial analyses, lease negotiations, and sometimes even development projects.

In my early career, I worked for a well-established brokerage firm where I was fortunate enough to observe some of the industry's top brokers in action. They weren't just salespeople; they were problem-solvers and dealmakers who knew how to navigate complex transactions and bring parties together. They had an in-depth knowledge of their markets, from vacancy rates to rental trends and new developments, and could see opportunities where others didn't. I quickly learned that if I wanted to succeed, I needed to go beyond just facilitating deals—I had to understand what my clients needed and provide solutions that helped them achieve their goals.

For example, one of my first significant deals involved a struggling retail property where the owner was looking to sell quickly due to financial difficulties. The initial approach from most brokers was to focus on finding a buyer who would pay the highest price. However, after speaking with the owner, I realized that the real issue was a lack of stable tenants, which was driving down the property's value.

Instead of just listing the property, I advised the owner to implement a short-term leasing strategy that could attract local businesses with flexible lease terms. We filled the vacancies, stabilized the income, and then marketed the property at a much higher valuation. That deal taught me that understanding a client's true objectives and having the creativity to address underlying problems can set you apart in this business.

Licensing and Training: The First Steps

Becoming a licensed commercial real estate broker is the first formal step in building your career. Licensing requirements vary by state but generally involve completing a set number of academic hours in real estate principles, passing a licensing exam, and practical experience by working under a licensed broker for a certain period. It's important to choose a brokerage firm that offers mentorship and training opportunities, especially when you're starting out. The guidance and advice you receive from experienced brokers can be invaluable. Don't focus on the size of the firm but instead focus on the professionals you will be working with and the mentorship opportunities available.

When I first joined the industry, I opted to work for a firm where I could work as a junior broker for a successful and ambitious broker which had more work than she could handle at the time. She trained me and provided me with a strong foundation in real estate, finance, leasing, sales, and market analysis. Aside from the formal training, it was the informal mentorship from other seasoned brokers that really helped me round out my practical, hands-on education. A couple of brokers in the office also had small commercial real estate investments and they taught me how to evaluate properties not just as buildings, but as income-generating assets, each with its own unique characteristics and potential.

According to a study by the National Association of Realtors, mentorship and ongoing professional development are significant factors in the long-term success of real estate professionals. The brokers who invest in their education and seek out guidance early on tend to achieve higher earnings and are more likely to stay in the industry long term.

Finding Your Niche and Specializing

One of the biggest mistakes I see new brokers make is trying to be all things to all people. The commercial real estate industry is incredibly diverse, with numerous property types and transaction types, each requiring different skills and expertise. To build a successful career, it's crucial to find your niche—whether it's office leasing, retail sales, industrial properties, or multifamily investments—and focus on becoming an expert in that area.

When I started, I took on a variety of property types because I thought that would give me more opportunities. However, I quickly realized that spreading myself too thin meant I wasn't developing deep expertise in any one area. I decided to specialize in office properties, specifically in emerging markets within Miami. This decision allowed me to build a detailed knowledge of office leasing trends, an understanding of what companies were looking for in workspace solutions, and allowed me to stay ahead of local market developments. By narrowing my focus, I became the go-to broker for businesses seeking office space in those areas. Specializing doesn't mean turning down every opportunity that doesn't fit your niche, but it does mean prioritizing your time and efforts to build a reputation in a specific segment.

The Importance of Personal Branding

In commercial real estate, your reputation is your brand. I learned early on that I had to be intentional about how I presented myself, both online and in person. Networking events, industry conferences, and even social media became important platforms for me to build my personal brand and demonstrate my expertise.

To stand out as a broker, you need to establish yourself as a trusted advisor. This goes beyond just selling properties—it's about providing value to your clients even when they're not in the market to buy or sell. I began writing articles for local business journals, sharing insights on market trends, and offering tips on commercial leasing strategies. This not only positioned me as a knowledgeable professional but also kept me top-of-mind for clients who might need my services in the future.

Personal branding does not focus solely on self-promotion. It also entails consistency and authenticity. Make sure that the way you present yourself online matches how you interact with people in real life. Clients appreciate honesty, and a genuine approach and this can differentiate you in a competitive industry.

Growing Your Network and Building Relationships

Networking is one of the most critical aspects of succeeding in commercial real estate. The deals you close and the clients you serve often come from relationships you've cultivated over time. When I first started, I was attending every industry event I could find—luncheons, association meetings, and real estate conferences. At first, it felt overwhelming, but it soon became clear how important those connections were.

The most valuable relationships I've built weren't necessarily with high-profile investors or large corporate clients. Some of the most beneficial connections were with other brokers, property managers, and even contractors who shared insights and referred clients. I once closed a significant deal thanks to a referral from a property manager who I had helped with a small leasing project years earlier. That connection led to an opportunity to list a multi-million-dollar property that otherwise would never have crossed my desk.

Networking is more than just exchanging business cards; it's about building genuine relationships based on mutual respect and shared interests. Whenever possible, I tried to give something back to my contacts, whether it was sharing market insights, introducing them to potential clients, or offering help with a project. Over time, these small gestures created a network of people who were eager to work with me and refer business my way.

Breaking into Brokerage: Working for a Firm vs. Starting Your Own

At some point in your brokerage career, you may face the decision of whether to stay with a brokerage firm or venture out and start your own. Each path has its benefits and challenges, and I've had the opportunity to experience both.

Working for an established firm can provide stability, resources, and a steady flow of leads, especially when you're starting out. I benefited greatly from the mentorship, training, and support that came with working for a well-known brokerage in my early career. It helped me learn the business and build a client base before I had the confidence to branch out on my own.

However, after a decade of working for others, there came a time when I wanted more control over my deals and more freedom to pursue opportunities that weren't always aligned with the firm's focus. Starting my own brokerage was a big leap, but it allowed me to build a brand that reflected my vision and gave me the flexibility to grow the business in ways that suited my strengths. It wasn't without its challenges; running your own brokerage meant handling all aspects of the business, from administrative tasks to compliance. It comes with much greater risk, including lawsuits for every person who works at your firm still, but the reward was the ability to help my clients and partners in a way I felt would benefit them the most and ultimately benefit me after helping them reach their goals.

Mastering the Art of Negotiation

Commercial real estate transactions often involve complex negotiations, especially when it comes to leasing or purchasing large properties. To be a successful broker, you need to develop strong negotiation skills. This means understanding not just your client's goals but also the motivations of the other parties involved. The goal of a negotiation is not always to "win" but to find a solution where all parties feel that they've gained something of value.

There is no successful negotiation if the other side is interested in only them winning and you losing. If that is the case, immediately move on as it will never result in a good deal for either party.

I remember one deal where the negotiations reached a stalemate but there was an interested buyer and seller. The seller refused to lower the price, and the buyer was unwilling to offer more. After speaking with both parties separately, I realized the seller's hesitation was rooted in concerns about future tax liabilities from the sale, while the buyer was worried about the property's need for repairs. By structuring the deal to include a seller's credit for repairs, coupled with a deferred payment structure, we addressed both concerns and were able to close the transaction. It was a reminder that successful negotiations often require creativity and an understanding of the underlying interests driving the positions of both sides. I believe in win/win deals and most of my career I have been involved in those transactions. Remember that sometimes you must walk away if that is not possible. You can't do good business with bad people.

Leveraging Data and Technology

As technology continues to evolve, so does the real estate industry. Data analytics, customer relationship management (CRM) systems, and market research tools have become indispensable for brokers who want to stay competitive. Early in my career, I realized the importance of using data not just for market analysis but also to enhance my client presentations and support my recommendations.

For instance, when advising a client on leasing strategies, I would use data on local market trends, such as rental rates, vacancy rates, and absorption rates, to justify my suggested rental terms. By providing data-driven insights, I was able to build credibility with clients and differentiate myself from brokers who relied solely on intuition.

Moreover, CRM systems allowed me to keep track of client interactions, follow up at the right times, and maintain relationships more effectively. The technology didn't replace personal connections, but enhanced by capabilities by helping me stay organized and ensure that I didn't miss any opportunities.

CHAPTER 5

Cutting-Edge Marketing—Outproducing Your Competition with Modern Strategies

In today's commercial real estate market, simply listing a property or putting up a "For Lease" sign isn't enough to attract the right tenants or buyers. The game has changed, and to stay ahead, you need to embrace modern marketing strategies. I've seen firsthand how adopting new marketing approaches can make a significant difference in the success of a property. It's more than having a digital presence—it's about using the right tools, creating engaging content, and consistently reaching your target audience.

When I first started, marketing a property meant taking out ads in newspapers and distributing printed brochures. While those methods still have some place in certain markets, they don't compare to the power of digital marketing and content creation today. The first time I truly embraced digital marketing was with a mixed-use development that had struggled to attract interest. We had beautiful professional photos, and our property descriptions were top-notch, but the leads were minimal. It wasn't until we started experimenting with social media, video content, and email campaigns that we saw a significant uptick in inquiries and foot traffic. That experience changed my perspective on what it means to "market" a property.

The Power of Digital Marketing in Commercial Real Estate

Digital marketing has transformed the real estate industry. It offers a way to reach a broader audience, engage potential clients in real time, and showcase properties like never before. For commercial real estate, this means utilizing websites, social media platforms, email campaigns, and even online events to connect with prospective tenants or buyers.

I remember a time when I was trying to lease a large office space in a competitive market. Traditional methods like print ads weren't generating enough interest, so I decided to overhaul our marketing strategy. We created a dedicated landing page for the property, complete with high-quality photos, a virtual tour, and a 3D floor plan. Additionally, we invested in social media ads that targeted business owners and companies looking for new office space in the area. Within a few weeks, interest surged, and we secured a new tenant for the building. This experience demonstrated that having a strong digital presence can make all the difference in attracting the right audience. But once you attract them, you need to focus on understanding their needs and building a relationship. Deals don't get done just by advertising and sending emails.

According to the National Association of Realtors, 87% of commercial real estate professionals say that digital marketing and online platforms have significantly increased their ability to attract quality leads. The modern buyer or tenant expects a seamless digital experience that provides information quickly and effectively, which is why having a robust digital marketing strategy is no longer optional—it's essential.

Using Social Media to Build Your Brand and Market Properties

Social media has become one of the most powerful tools for marketing commercial real estate. Platforms like LinkedIn, Instagram, and even TikTok have opened up new channels to connect with prospects, showcase properties, and build a personal brand. When used correctly, social media can help you outproduce your competition by creating an ongoing conversation with your audience.

Early on, I was hesitant to use social media for commercial properties. I saw it as a platform for lifestyle content and didn't think it could add much value to real estate. But as I observed others having success, I decided to give it a try. One of the first campaigns I ran was for a retail center which had undergone significant renovation. We launched a series of posts showcasing the updated design, tenant mix, and community events. We used Instagram Stories to highlight tenant features, LinkedIn to share market trends and insights, and Facebook for event promotions. The response was impressive; we saw a marked increase in tenant inquiries and even gained media coverage through a local business journal that picked up our campaign.

Social media doesn't just work for large-scale campaigns—it's also highly effective for smaller, more personal content. Sharing behind-the-scenes stories, updates on new listings, or even short videos explaining market trends can position you as an expert in your niche. For example, I began posting short, informative videos on LinkedIn, where I would share my thoughts on local market trends or tips for first-time commercial investors. These posts not only helped me connect with my existing network but also brought in new leads who had never heard of me before. Social media allows you to create an ongoing dialogue with your audience, build credibility, and stay top-of-mind.

Creating Engaging Content: Virtual Tours, Videos, and Podcasts

Content is king when it comes to digital marketing. In commercial real estate, it's not enough to have a listing on a website; you need to create content that tells a story, engages viewers, and makes them want to learn more. This could include virtual property tours, informative videos, podcasts, or blog articles.

One of the most impactful changes I made to my marketing approach was incorporating video content. A few years ago, I had a large industrial property to lease that was located on the outskirts of the city. It wasn't the most attractive property on paper, and we struggled to generate interest from traditional marketing efforts. I decided to produce a video that showcased the property's strengths—its large loading docks, upgraded facilities, and proximity to major highways. We included drone footage to provide a unique perspective and highlighted the property's convenient access to interstate highways. The video not only helped us lease the space but also became an asset that we used in other marketing campaigns.

Videos aren't just limited to property tours; they can also be used to educate your audience. I've found that sharing videos in which I explain the benefits of different emerging markets and market trends attracted a lot of attention which can lead to introductions to new clients. According to research by HubSpot, 54% of consumers prefer to see more video content from brands they support, which underscores the power of video in marketing.

Podcasts are another great way to engage with your audience. I started hosting a podcast where I discussed commercial real estate trends, interviewed industry experts, and shared insights on different aspects of investing. Not only did this help me reach a wider audience, but it also positioned me as a thought leader in the industry. I noticed that potential clients who listened to my podcast were more informed about market conditions and already viewed me as a trusted advisor before even meeting in person.

Leveraging AI and Data-Driven Marketing

Artificial Intelligence (AI) has rapidly become a game-changer in marketing. In commercial real estate, AI can be used to analyze market data, automate email campaigns, segment customers, and predict trends. Incorporating AI into your marketing strategy can help you *target the right audience* more effectively and personalize your marketing efforts.

I first experimented with AI when I was trying to market a property that was suitable for a variety of tenants—from retail businesses to office users. We used AI-driven software to analyze data on businesses that had recently opened in the area, cross-referencing that information with companies that had recently raised funding or announced expansions. We then used this data to create a targeted email campaign and social media ads directed specifically at those businesses. The result was an increase in qualified leads, as we were reaching prospects who were actively looking for new space. According to the Commercial Real Estate Finance Council, data-driven marketing strategies that use AI can increase lead conversion rates by up to 30%.

Another advantage of using AI is for *content creation*. I've used AI-powered tools to generate property descriptions, automate social media posts, and even help with market research. While AI shouldn't replace the human touch in marketing, it can certainly make the process more efficient and allow you to focus on high-level strategies.

Repurposing Content Across Multiple Platforms

One of the best ways to maximize your marketing efforts is by repurposing content. This means taking a piece of content, such as a blog post or video, and adapting it for use across different platforms. For example, if I create a detailed market report for my website, I can also break it down into several shorter social media posts, record a podcast episode discussing the report, and even create an infographic that highlights the key findings. Repurposing content allows you to reach different audiences while keeping your message consistent.

A case in point was when I produced a video about trends in the local office market. The original video was posted on LinkedIn, where it performed well. To expand its reach, I edited the content into shorter clips for Instagram, created a blog post summarizing the points covered in the video, and used some of the footage to create a virtual tour of one of the office spaces I was marketing. This multi-channel approach resulted in higher engagement across platforms and generated more inquiries than if I had only used the video in one place.

Case Study: How a Content-Heavy Approach Outperformed the Competition

I once worked with a client who owned a Class B office building in an area dominated by newer, Class A properties. The competition was fierce, and our traditional marketing efforts weren't generating enough traction. We decided to take a content-heavy approach to set the property apart from the competition.

We started by producing a series of videos that showcased not just the building but also the surrounding area, highlighting local amenities, the walkability of the neighborhood, and transportation options. We complemented the videos with blog posts that discussed market trends, the benefits of choosing a Class B space over Class A, and tips for businesses looking to downsize without compromising quality. We even hosted a webinar on the future of office space in a post-pandemic world, using the property as an example of flexible office solutions.

This comprehensive content strategy created a narrative around the property that appealed to our target market—small to medium-sized businesses looking for affordable yet high-quality office space. Within months, we saw an increase in leasing activity and were able to fill the vacancies more quickly than expected. The content-driven approach not only helped us lease the property but also strengthened the building's brand in the market.

Staying Consistent and Measuring Your Success

No marketing strategy is complete without consistent execution and performance measurement. One of the most common mistakes I see in commercial real estate is inconsistency. Brokers and property managers often start a marketing campaign with a lot of enthusiasm, but then let it fizzle out. Marketing requires ongoing effort and attention to detail.

For every campaign, I set specific goals, such as the number of leads generated or engagement metrics for social media. I use analytics tools to track the performance of my content and adjust as needed. For example, if a particular video isn't getting the expected number of views, I may change the title, update the thumbnail, or promote it on a different platform. By continuously measuring success and adjusting tactics, I ensure that my marketing efforts stay on track.

The Future of Marketing in Commercial Real Estate

The landscape of commercial real estate marketing continues to evolve, and staying ahead of the curve is crucial. As more platforms and tools become available, there are endless possibilities for reaching potential tenants and buyers. In the future, I believe that immersive experiences such as augmented reality (AR) and virtual reality (VR) tours will become standard for high-end properties, allowing prospects to explore spaces from anywhere in the world. Embracing these innovations early can give you a competitive edge and help you stand out in a crowded market.

CHAPTER 6

Common Pitfalls in Commercial Real Estate—and How to Avoid Them

Commercial real estate can be a highly rewarding industry, but it is also fraught with risks and challenges. The journey to success in this field is rarely straightforward, and even the most seasoned investors and brokers encounter setbacks along the way. Early in my career, I made plenty of mistakes that cost me time and money, but each one taught me valuable lessons that helped shape my approach to real estate today. Knowing what pitfalls to avoid can make the difference between a profitable investment and a costly misstep.

There are many uncontrollable's in all businesses: Interest rates, litigation, fraud, the broader economy, but the key is trying to focus on the items that are within your control.

I've seen a wide range of mistakes, from overestimating potential returns to neglecting crucial due diligence. However, the good news is that many of these pitfalls can be mitigated—or even avoided altogether—with careful planning, realistic expectations, and a willingness to adapt. Here, I'll share some of the most common pitfalls in commercial real estate and how to steer clear of them.

Mistake #1: Overestimating Potential Profits

It's easy to get caught up in the excitement of a new investment, especially when it seems like a "sure thing." Early in my career, I found myself making overly optimistic projections about a property's potential returns. I'd calculate the rental income based on ideal conditions, with full occupancy and high rental rates, while underestimating the likelihood of vacancies, maintenance expenses, or unexpected repairs. The reality sometimes fell short of my expectations.

For example, one of my investments was a small retail strip center in a busy area of Miami. It seemed like a no-brainer at the time, with high foot traffic and solid tenants in place. I calculated the returns based on a 95% occupancy rate and anticipated rental increases, but within a year, two of the tenants left due to business closures, and I struggled to fill those vacancies. The income I had projected evaporated quickly, and the carrying costs began to add up.

The lesson here is to always use conservative estimates when projecting potential profits. It's better to assume lower occupancy rates, more modest rent increases, and higher operating expenses than to be caught off guard. As a rule of thumb, I now calculate a property's expected cash flow based on a vacancy rate of at least

10%, even if the current occupancy is higher. This approach helps build a buffer for potential downturns or unexpected events.

According to the Real Estate Finance Journal, 35% of first-time commercial real estate investors report that their initial projections were overly optimistic due to underestimating expenses and overestimating rental income. By setting realistic expectations, you'll avoid financial strain and be better positioned to manage the property effectively.

Mistake #2: Neglecting Thorough Due Diligence

One of the most critical aspects of any real estate transaction is due diligence. This process involves a thorough investigation of the property's condition, market, legal status, and financials. Skipping or rushing through due diligence is one of the quickest ways to end up with a problematic property.

I recall a deal where I was eager to close on an industrial building because it seemed like an incredible bargain. The seller was motivated, and the location was favorable for logistics. However, I didn't pay enough attention to the environmental reports, assuming that any issues would be minor. At the last minute, before my deposit became non-refundable, I discovered that the property had significant soil contamination that required costly remediation. The best deals are sometimes the ones you walk away from. If I had closed on the property, the discount I thought I was getting would have been quickly dwarfed by the cleanup expenses.

To avoid these pitfalls, you must be meticulous in your due diligence and assemble a team of professionals who are subject matter experts including environmental inspection firms; engineers, attorneys and even bankers who have seen all the pitfalls of other deals over their careers. Proper due diligence includes everything from environmental assessments and structural inspections to zoning regulations and existing lease agreements. Due diligence should be performed on the condition of the property, the legal, and the financial aspects of the potential project. The Building Owners and Managers Association (BOMA) advises conducting a comprehensive property condition assessment (PCA) before purchasing any commercial property. This assessment helps identify potential risks and informs your decision-making process. It's essential to hire reputable professionals to assist in these evaluations, as their expertise can uncover issues that aren't immediately visible to you but will be to an expert.

Mistake #3: Misjudging Market Timing

Market timing is an essential factor in commercial real estate, but it's often overlooked by eager investors who rush into deals without considering broader economic trends. While it's true that real estate markets are cyclical, predicting the exact timing of a market peak or trough is nearly impossible. However, being aware of market conditions and understanding where you are in the cycle can guide your investment decisions. You can't fight the market. A great property in a bad market is still a poor investment.

I once made the mistake of buying a property at the height of a real estate boom. The prices were high, and competition for deals was fierce, but I didn't want to miss out. I purchased an office building in a prominent suburb with high occupancy in an area that was rapidly gentrifying, expecting the growth to continue. Unfortunately, the market cooled off shortly after, and leasing defaults occurred almost immediately. I struggled to fill vacancies and had to offer substantial concessions to attract tenants. The lesson here was clear: just because a market is hot doesn't mean it's the right time to buy.

A better approach is to focus on properties with strong fundamentals and limited downside, by buying at a discount and if that's not available, then sitting on the sidelines and waiting. , Look for well-located properties with stable tenant bases, reasonable pricing relative to comparable sales, and value-add potential that isn't dependent on market appreciation. The Urban Land Institute's report on market cycles suggests that while timing plays a role, successful investors prioritize properties that can weather different market conditions.

Mistake #4: Ignoring the Importance of Property Management

Once you've acquired a property, effective management is crucial for maintaining its value and generating consistent income. It's easy to assume that managing a commercial property is a straightforward process, but in reality, it requires strong execution, careful attention to tenant needs, rigorous budget controls, maintenance, and financial management. Failing to prioritize property management can lead to tenant turnover, deteriorating conditions, and financial losses.

Early on, I managed one of my properties with an inexperienced property manager because I thought I could save on costs. I underestimated the amount of time and expertise needed to keep up with tenant requests, handle maintenance issues, and ensure the building operated efficiently. Eventually, tenant dissatisfaction led to vacancies, and I ended up spending more time and money trying to address the problems than if I had hired an experienced professional manager from the start.

To avoid this pitfall, consider hiring a property management firm if you are not set up to manage your own properties. According to a report by the Institute of Real Estate Management (IREM), professionally managed properties tend to have higher tenant retention rates and lower maintenance costs compared to those managed by inexperienced owners.

Mistake #5: Underestimating Capital Expenditures and Maintenance Costs

When calculating the potential returns on a property, it's essential to account for capital expenditures (CapEx) and ongoing maintenance costs. These expenses can vary significantly depending on the property's age, condition, and intended use. Neglecting to budget adequately for these costs can quickly turn a profitable investment into a financial burden.

I learned this the hard way when I purchased an older office building that had not been updated in several years. I budgeted for minor repairs, but once I started renovating, I found that the HVAC needed replacement. Although we had "hoped" that the unit would last several years, we should have assumed the worst-case scenario. The cost of these upgrades far exceeded my initial estimates, significantly impacting on my cash flow.

The lesson here is that 'hope' is not a strategy and to always conduct a thorough inspection, budget for full capital expenditures in the first year and don't assume that you can get by for a while without the capex investment. The Real Estate Finance Journal recommends setting aside at least 10% to 15% of annual gross income for CapEx reserves, especially for older properties. This reserve can help cover unexpected repairs or upgrades without straining the property's finances.

Mistake #6: Failing to Adapt to Changing Market Trends

The commercial real estate market is continuously evolving, influenced by factors such as technological advancements, demographic shifts, and economic changes. Failing to adapt to these trends can leave investors and brokers at a disadvantage. For instance, the increasing demand for flexible office space and remote work options has reshaped the office leasing market. Properties that haven't adapted to these trends may struggle to attract tenants.

A few years ago, I managed a traditional office building that was struggling to maintain occupancy. Instead of continuing with the same leasing strategy, I adapted by converting some of the suites into flexible workspaces and offering shorter lease terms to accommodate startups and small businesses. This change attracted a new tenant demographic and increased the building's appeal in a market that was shifting toward more flexible work arrangements.

To stay competitive, it's crucial to monitor industry trends and be willing to adjust your approach. This could mean offering more flexible lease terms, incorporating smart building technologies, or even repurposing a property for a different use. The National Real Estate Investor reports that properties that adapt to emerging trends tend to have higher occupancy rates and are better positioned to capitalize on future growth opportunities.

Mistake #7: Not Understanding the Needs of Your Tenants

A property's success largely depends on its tenants. If you don't take the time to understand what your tenants need and how your property can serve those needs, you risk losing them to competitors who offer better solutions. I've seen property owners make the mistake of focusing solely on rent increases without considering tenant satisfaction. The result is often increased turnover and higher vacancy rates.

In one of my properties, I struggled to retain tenants despite offering competitive rental rates. After conducting tenant surveys and speaking directly with some of the businesses, I learned that the main issue was a lack of amenities and outdated common areas. By investing in a few upgrades, such as adding a fitness center and modernizing the lobby, I was able to improve tenant retention significantly. I thought their rent cost was the most important item at that time, but my tenants taught me that it was the value they were receiving for their rental payments and not just the financial aspect.

The Institute of Real Estate Management recommends regularly gathering feedback from tenants and using that information to make improvements that enhance tenant satisfaction. This approach not only helps retain existing tenants but also attracts new ones.

CHAPTER 7

Leveraging Relationships —Networking and Partnerships in Real Estate

Commercial real estate is often considered a relationship-driven business, and for good reason. While knowledge, analysis, and negotiation skills are critical, the people you connect with can open doors to opportunities that might otherwise be inaccessible. Early in my career, I realized that the deals I closed, the properties I managed, and the investments I made were all influenced by the relationships I built along the way.

Successful real estate professionals understand that relationships are more than just business transactions; they are partnerships that require mutual respect, trust, and shared value. From collaborating with other brokers and forming alliances with investors to connecting with contractors and government officials, your network is a powerful asset that can accelerate your career and enhance your investments. In this chapter, I'll share some of the key principles and strategies that have helped me cultivate valuable relationships and leverage them to grow my business.

The Power of Relationships in Real Estate

The real estate industry is built on people. Whether you're dealing with buyers, sellers, tenants, lenders, or contractors, the relationships you foster play a significant role in the success of your projects. I've always found that the most rewarding deals I've been a part of weren't just about the numbers—they were about the people involved. The trust I had built with my clients and partners helped create an environment where deals could be executed more smoothly, negotiations could be handled more openly, and problems could be solved more efficiently.

One of the earliest lessons I learned was the value of cultivating long-term relationships rather than focusing solely on short-term gains. I remember a deal where I was negotiating on behalf of a client to purchase a large office property. During the negotiations, we encountered an issue with the property's zoning, which could have derailed the entire transaction. Instead of playing hardball and risking a standoff, I took the time to communicate directly with the seller's broker, with whom I had worked on several deals in the past. Because we had a good working relationship, we were able to resolve the issue amicably and find a solution that worked for both parties. This experience taught me that a strong network can be the key to navigating unexpected challenges.

Building a Real Estate Network

Networking is broader than collecting business cards or attending industry events; it's about building meaningful connections that can add value to your career or investments. I have always prioritized quality over quantity when it comes to my network. It's more effective to have a few strong relationships that you can rely on than a long list of acquaintances you barely know.

When I first started in the industry, I attended nearly every real estate event, conference, and seminar I could find. At first, it felt overwhelming and even intimidating, especially when I was surrounded by more experienced professionals. But I quickly learned that networking wasn't just about introducing myself to as many people as possible—it was about having genuine conversations and finding common ground. I focused on establishing connections with people who shared similar interests or were involved in aspects of the industry that I wanted to learn more about. This approach allowed me to form deeper, more meaningful relationships, which became valuable sources of advice, referrals, and opportunities.

Over time, I realized that the key to networking is not just about getting to know people but also entails staying relevant and top-of-mind. I make it a habit to stay in touch with my contacts regularly, whether it's through a quick catch-up call, sharing an interesting article, or meeting up for coffee. The National Real Estate Investor suggests that maintaining regular communication with your network is crucial for staying relevant and for creating new business opportunities that may arise from casual conversations.

Strategic Partnerships: Creating Value Together

In commercial real estate, partnerships can take many forms, from joint ventures and syndications to strategic alliances with service providers or contractors. I've always believed that the right partnership can add tremendous value to a project by bringing in complementary skills, additional capital, or a fresh perspective. However, finding the right partner is not always easy. It requires aligning interests, setting clear expectations, and building trust.

One of my most successful partnerships came about when I was working on a mixed-use development. I had the vision for the project but needed additional financing and expertise to get it off the ground. I partnered with an investor who had experience with similar projects and brought valuable connections in the local government. By working together, we were able to secure the necessary permits, attract reputable tenants, and complete the project on time and under budget. This experience highlighted the importance of choosing partners who bring something unique to the table and share your commitment to the project's success.

When considering a partnership, it's essential to establish a clear structure from the outset. Outline each party's responsibilities, contributions, and expected returns. The Urban Land Institute advises that joint venture agreements should include detailed terms on decision-making authority, profit distribution, exit strategies, and conflict resolution mechanisms. This clarity helps prevent misunderstandings and ensures that all parties are aligned toward a common goal.

You will only find out the true character of a partner after something goes wrong. If at all possible, try to find out how your potential partner acted when a deal didn't go well.

Attending Industry Events: Networking with Purpose

Industry events, conferences, and trade shows can be valuable opportunities to expand your network, learn about market trends, and generate new business leads. However, attending these events without a plan can be a waste of time. I've always found that having a specific objective for each event—whether it's to meet potential clients, learn about new investment opportunities, or reconnect with old contacts—helps me get the most out of my attendance.

For example, when I attended my first International Council of Shopping Centers (ICSC) conference, I was relatively new to the retail property investment sector. Instead of trying to network with everyone, I focused on attending sessions that dealt with trends in retail development and sought out conversations with developers who were actively working on similar projects. This targeted approach not only helped me make valuable connections but also gave me insights that I later applied to my own retail investments.

To maximize the impact of industry events, it's important to follow up afterward. Sending a quick email or LinkedIn message to the people you met can help solidify the connection and set the stage for future collaboration. Research from the Real Estate Marketing Association indicates that attendees who follow up with new contacts within a week of an event are 60% more likely to establish long-term relationships compared to those who wait longer.

The Role of Mentors and Advisors

Throughout my career, mentors played a crucial role in my development as a real estate professional. A mentor can offer guidance, share valuable experiences, and even open doors to new opportunities. Early in my career, I sought out mentors who had already achieved the kind of success I aspired to. These individuals helped me navigate complex transactions, introduced me to key contacts, and provided a sounding board for my ideas.

One of my most important mentors was an experienced broker who taught me the art of negotiation. He explained that it wasn't simply closing deals; it was about understanding the motivations of the other parties and finding ways to create win-win situations. This lesson stayed with me and has been a guiding principle in my approach to real estate. Over time, I've also made it a priority to give back, by mentoring younger professionals who are just starting in the industry. Not only does this help them, but it also keeps me engaged and connected with the next generation of talent.

According to the National Association of Realtors, real estate professionals who work with mentors are 70% more likely to achieve higher earnings and career satisfaction compared to those who don't seek mentorship. Mentorship offers an invaluable resource for navigating the complexities of the industry and avoiding costly mistakes.

Building a Network Beyond Real Estate

While having a strong network within the real estate industry is essential, I've found that expanding your network beyond the field can offer unexpected benefits. Connections in other industries—such as finance, law, construction, or technology—can provide insights, referrals, or even lead to new business opportunities.

For instance, I once partnered with a technology entrepreneur who was looking to invest in real estate. While his primary business wasn't in real estate, his knowledge of technology helped us integrate smart building features into a new office development, making it more appealing to modern tenants. This partnership gave me access to a different set of resources and perspectives that enhanced the overall value of the project.

I recommend actively seeking out networking events, seminars, or social groups outside of real estate. Attending events that focus on business, entrepreneurship, or even civic engagement can help you meet people who may eventually have a real estate need, or who could be valuable partners in a future project.

Turning Contacts into Collaborators

Having a network of contacts is one thing but turning those contacts into collaborators who are willing to invest time, resources, or money into your projects requires a strategic approach. I've always believed in nurturing relationships by offering value first. When you're generous with your time, advice, or connections, people are more likely to reciprocate and collaborate when opportunities arise.

I once had a contact who owned several retail properties. We have stayed in touch over the years, sharing market insights and occasionally referring clients to one another. When a redevelopment opportunity came up for a retail center in need of revitalization, I reached out to him to see if he'd be interested in partnering on the project. He said he didn't want a partner, but he would hire me for the purchase and the leasing, and property management. It was because we had a strong foundation of trust and mutual benefit, he was eager to find a way we could both benefit even if it was not the way I originally envisioned.

Research by the Real Estate Finance Journal shows that real estate professionals who engage in collaborative projects with their contacts are more likely to achieve higher returns on investment compared to those who work alone. The key is to approach partnerships with a mindset of creating value for everyone involved.

Giving Back to the Community and Building Goodwill

Being involved in the community is another way to strengthen your network and create goodwill. Community involvement is not just about increasing your visibility, it also provides opportunities to connect with like-minded individuals who share similar values. I've been involved in various community initiatives, from supporting local schools, sitting on charitable boards, raising money in capital campaigns for non-profits, volunteering at my church and sponsoring charity events. This involvement has helped me form relationships with local leaders, business owners, and even potential clients who have shared values.

One of the most impactful experiences I had was assisting with a nonprofit organization that provided affordable housing to low-income families. I volunteered my time to help secure properties and facilitate renovations. Not only did this project fulfill a personal desire to give back, but it also expanded my network to include philanthropists, social workers, and government officials. This experience led to a two-decade love of building workforce multifamily apartments for working people in our community.

The Building Owners and Managers Association (BOMA) reports that companies and professionals who engage in community service and corporate social responsibility initiatives often see higher levels of brand loyalty and customer retention. This goodwill can translate into a stronger reputation and a more robust network of supporters and collaborators. But we do it, and so should you, because it makes you feel good to help others.

CHAPTER 8

Long-Term Success in Commercial Real Estate

Commercial real estate is not a short-term game. It's an industry where lasting success is built over years, even decades, with careful planning, strategic decision-making, and continuous adaptation. Many people enter the business hoping to strike it rich quickly, but I've found that the most successful real estate investors and brokers take a long-term approach. They understand that the real wealth in commercial real estate comes from sustained growth, compounded returns, and the ability to navigate through various market cycles.

I learned early on that the key to long-term success is having a clear vision, staying disciplined in your approach, and being prepared to adapt as conditions change. Everyone who is in our industry has setbacks and challenges but those that fight through those challenges and face them head on, instead of running to a different industry, are the ones that create long term success. Commercial real estate is a dynamic industry influenced by economic trends, evolving market demands, and regulatory changes. Those who can anticipate shifts and adjust their strategies accordingly will not only survive but thrive in the long run.

Reinvesting Profits for Continued Growth

One of the most critical decisions you'll make as a real estate investor is what to do with the profits from your properties. It's tempting to take the gains and spend them on personal luxuries, but if you want to build a truly substantial portfolio, you need to reinvest those profits wisely. Early in my career, I made it a point to reinvest a significant portion of my earnings back into new deals, property improvements, or debt reduction.

However, in 2008 all those reinvestments went up in smoke. Consequently, I believe that the first profits should go to cash reserves to provide a cushion in a downturn and then they should go towards paying down principal on debt. The most successful real estate investors are not the ones who make high returns with high debt ratios but the ones who have low or no debt and consistent cash flow. Also, another important element of reinvesting profits are the tax implications of investing.

For example, after selling an apartment building for a substantial profit, I had the choice of either cashing out or using the proceeds in a 1031 tax free exchange to acquire another property. Instead of spending the profits, I reinvested them into a value-add multifamily project that needed renovations. The increased rental income from the renovated units significantly boosted the property's value, allowing me to refinance and pull-out additional equity, tax free again, for future investments. This process of reinvesting, refinancing and using tax free or tax advantaged investment proceeds has become a cornerstone of my strategy for building long-term wealth in real estate.

The Real Estate Finance Journal suggests that reinvesting profits into higher-yield properties, renovations, or paying down debt can lead to compounded returns over time. The key is to strike a balance between taking profits in the short term and reinvesting for the long term, ensuring that your portfolio continues to grow without becoming over-leveraged and taking advantage of tax benefits for commercial real estate

Understanding and Managing Market Cycles

Commercial real estate markets are cyclical, with periods of growth followed by slowdowns or downturns. Understanding these cycles and positioning yourself accordingly can make a significant difference in your long-term success. I've experienced several market cycles throughout my career, from the boom years of the early 2000s to the financial crisis of 2008 and the recovery that followed. Each cycle taught me valuable lessons about managing risk, seizing opportunities, and staying resilient.

During periods of economic expansion, it's easy to get caught up in the enthusiasm and overpay for properties. I remember buying an office building in a rapidly growing market just before the 2008 downturn. The property seemed like a fantastic deal at the time, with a strong demand for office space and rising rents. However, when the recession hit, leasing activity slowed dramatically, and I struggled to maintain occupancy. This experience taught me the importance of not overextending during boom times and always having a contingency plan in place for economic downturns.

Conversely, downturns can present some of the best opportunities for growth. When property values decline and competition decreases, savvy investors can acquire assets at discounted prices. In the years following the 2008 crisis, I was able to purchase distressed properties for clients at a fraction of their previous values. By making strategic improvements and waiting for the market to recover, I was able to significantly increase the value of those assets. This taught me that the most successful investors keep dry powder and cash on the sidelines for opportunistic purchases at a discount.

The Urban Land Institute emphasizes the importance of understanding market cycles and suggests that successful investors focus on properties with strong fundamentals that can withstand different phases of the cycle. Additionally, maintaining liquidity during boom periods can provide the flexibility needed to take advantage of opportunities during downturns.

Diversifying Your Portfolio

Diversification is a common strategy in many forms of investing, and commercial real estate is no exception. While it's important to specialize and become an expert in a particular property type, it's also wise to diversify your portfolio to mitigate risk. Early in my career, I primarily focused on office properties, but as my business grew, I began to explore other sectors such as retail, industrial, and multifamily. This diversification not only helped me spread risk but also allowed me to capitalize on trends in different markets.

For instance, when the office market experienced a downturn due to economic shifts, my industrial properties, which were benefiting from the rise of e-commerce, helped offset the decline. Similarly, multifamily properties tend to perform well during recessions, as people look for more affordable housing options. By having a diversified portfolio, I was able to weather market fluctuations more effectively and maintain steady cash flow.

According to the National Real Estate Investor, a diversified real estate portfolio can provide more stable returns over time and reduce the impact of downturns in any single property type. The goal is to balance your portfolio across different asset classes, geographic locations, and investment strategies.

Creating a Legacy in Real Estate

Long-term success in commercial real estate is not just about accumulating properties or achieving financial milestones; it's also about creating a legacy. Building a legacy means having a long-lasting impact on the community, mentoring the next generation of real estate professionals, and helping others achieve success for their families and the next generation.

One of the projects that I am most proud of was transforming apartment buildings for affordable housing in the Little Havane neighborhood of Miami. The building had been filled with disreputable tenants for years and was in complete disrepair. Many people saw it as an eyesore, but I saw an opportunity to breathe new life into it. I worked with my property manager and contractors, and local government officials to restore its historic charm while providing a quality affordable apartments for newer working immigrant families to live and begin their own American Dream. The redevelopment sparked additional investment in the neighborhood, and the area soon became a vibrant area with other investors buying older apartment buildings and restoring them.

Creating a legacy isn't just about big development projects; it can also be achieved by giving back to the community, supporting local causes, or mentoring young professionals who aspire to build careers in real estate. I've always made it a point to share my knowledge and experiences with others, whether through formal mentorship programs or informal advice sessions. The Building Owners and Managers Association (BOMA) suggests that real estate professionals who actively mentor others and engage in community service tend to have stronger networks and are more fulfilled in their careers.

Maintaining a Positive Attitude and Staying Motivated

Sustaining long-term success requires more than just a sound investment strategy; it also requires the right mindset. Real estate is a demanding industry that often involves setbacks, uncertainties, lawsuits and hard work. I've had my fair share of deals that didn't go as planned, tenants who vacated unexpectedly, and economic downturns that affected my portfolio. However, I've always found that maintaining a positive attitude, facing troubles head-on, showing up every day and working hard, providing more service than you are paid for and staying focused on long-term goals helped me navigate challenges and keep moving forward.

One of the habits I developed early on was setting both short-term and long-term goals. The short-term goals kept me motivated day-to-day, while the long-term goals helped me stay on track with my broader vision for success. For instance, when I was first starting, my short-term goal might have been to close a certain number of deals in a year, while my long-term goal was to build a portfolio that generated passive income.

Celebrating small wins along the way also helps maintain motivation. Each successful deal, even the smaller ones, is a step toward the bigger picture. Recognizing these accomplishments can provide the encouragement needed to tackle the next challenge. Research from the Real Estate Marketing Association indicates that setting achievable milestones and acknowledging progress can significantly improve job satisfaction and reduce burnout.

Adapting to Changing Market Conditions

The ability to adapt is perhaps one of the most important qualities for achieving long-term success in commercial real estate. The market is always changing due to factors such as technological advancements, shifting demographics, and evolving consumer preferences. Staying ahead of these changes requires a proactive approach to market research and a willingness to adjust your strategies as needed.

For example, the rise of remote work has transformed the office sector in recent years. Many companies have downsized their physical office spaces, while others have opted for flexible, co-working arrangements. To adapt, I began focusing on properties that offered flexible lease terms or could be converted into different uses. In some cases, I even reconfigured traditional office spaces to include shared amenities, such as conference rooms and lounges, to cater to tenants seeking a more flexible work environment.

Another example is the impact of e-commerce on retail properties. As more consumers shifted to online shopping, I saw opportunities to repurpose underperforming retail centers into mixed-use developments that included residential units, entertainment venues, and experiential retail. By staying adaptable and exploring creative solutions, I was able to turn potential challenges into profitable ventures for my partners, my clients and ultimately for myself.

The Urban Land Institute's reports on adaptive reuse suggest that the most successful investors are those who remain open to reimagining the use of their properties and staying attuned to emerging trends that could affect the real estate landscape.

Creating a Succession Plan for Your Real Estate Business

Planning isn't just about your properties; it's also about the future of your business. If you've built a successful real estate company, having a succession plan is crucial to ensure that the business continues to thrive even after you step back. I've seen many cases where real estate companies struggled or fell apart after the founder retired because there was no clear plan for leadership transition.

A solid succession plan involves identifying potential successors, whether they are family members, employees, or external candidates. It's important to start preparing them for leadership roles early, providing them with the necessary training and involving them in strategic decision-making. I've made it a point to involve my successors in major projects, allowing them to take on increasing levels of responsibility over time. This gradual transition has helped ensure that they are ready to take the reins when the time comes.

The National Real Estate Investor highlights that businesses with a well-defined succession plan are more likely to continue growing after a leadership change. This planning not only provides peace of mind but also enhances the company's reputation and stability.

CHAPTER 9

Leadership and Mindset —The Qualities of a Successful Investor

Success in commercial real estate goes beyond buying properties and closing deals. It requires a particular mindset and a set of qualities that help navigate the complexities of the market, overcome obstacles, and build lasting relationships. When I look back on my career, I realize that the skills and mindset I developed over the years were just as important as the strategies I employed. It entailed knowing more than just the numbers or understanding the market; it was about leading with integrity, staying resilient in the face of challenges, and continuously striving for growth.

Real estate is a business of people, and those who succeed in this industry are often the ones who can lead others, inspire confidence, and maintain a positive attitude even when things don't go as planned. In this chapter, I'll share some of the key qualities that I believe are essential for a successful investor and offer insights into how to cultivate them.

Developing a Leadership Mindset

Leadership in commercial real estate isn't about having a title or position; about it incorporates setting an example and influencing others to achieve a common goal. I learned this early in my career when I was managing a team for the first time. It was a small team, and we were working on a challenging redevelopment project. The building had multiple issues, including structural concerns and zoning complications, and the team was feeling overwhelmed. Instead of pushing everyone to work harder, I decided to take a step back and listen to their concerns. We had an open discussion about the challenges we faced and came up with a plan together. This approach not only boosted morale but also helped us find creative solutions that ultimately saved time and money.

I've found that effective leadership involves being present, approachable, and willing to listen. It's about empowering others to do their best work and fostering a culture where collaboration and innovation can thrive. The best leaders don't just give orders; they provide guidance, offer support, and lead by example.

Research from the Building Owners and Managers Association (BOMA) suggests that real estate professionals who adopt a leadership mindset and prioritize team development are more likely to achieve long-term success in their projects. A strong leader can motivate others to go above and beyond, even in difficult situations.

Embracing Resilience in the Face of Challenges

Commercial real estate is not without its ups and downs. There will be times when deals fall through, partners will disappoint you, tenants default on leases, or unexpected expenses arise. The difference between successful investors and those who give up is resilience—the ability to bounce back from setbacks and keep moving forward. According to one of my hero's, General George S. Patton: "Success is how high you bounce when you hit bottom"

I recall a time when I was in the middle of renovating an apartment property, and the main contractor went bankrupt halfway through the project. The situation was dire; the construction was halted, the budget was stretched thin, and there was no immediate solution in sight. I could have panicked or walked away from the project, but instead, I chose to face the situation head-on. I quickly found a replacement contractor, renegotiated terms with the subcontractors, and restructured the budget to complete the project. It wasn't easy, and I never made money on the project, but I didn't lose any either, and we turned lemons and a potential big loss into lemonade and the opportunity to fight another day.

Resilience isn't just about enduring tough times; it's about learning from them and that's called experience. Each setback presents an opportunity to gain valuable insights and improve your approach. I've learned to see challenges as learning experiences that make me a stronger investor. The Urban Land Institute emphasizes the importance of resilience in real estate, noting that the most successful professionals view setbacks as temporary obstacles that can be overcome with persistence and problem-solving.

According to Louis L. Lafontissee II Esquire, a remarkable real estate attorney in Miami for over 65 Years and a Legend in our community: Oscar Wilde says, "Experience is the name we give to our mistakes".

Maintaining a Positive Attitude

A positive attitude can be a powerful tool in the world of real estate. There will be moments of uncertainty, and it's easy to become discouraged when things don't go as planned. However, maintaining a positive outlook can help you stay motivated, inspire your team, and attract opportunities.

I remember working on a complex lease negotiation for a large industrial space. The tenant was a major logistics company, and their requirements were extensive. Negotiations dragged on for months, and at one point, it seemed like the deal was going to fall apart. Instead of becoming frustrated, I chose to remain optimistic and focused on finding a way to address the tenant's concerns. We eventually reached an agreement, and the deal went through. This experience taught me that a positive mindset and a little bit of patience can help you stay committed and find solutions, even when the path forward is unclear.

According to a study published in the Real Estate Finance Journal, investors who maintain a positive mindset are more likely to make better decisions under pressure, as they are able to focus on solutions rather than problems. A positive attitude can also help attract like-minded partners, clients, and tenants who value optimism and persistence.

Cultivating Adaptability in a Changing Market

The commercial real estate market is constantly evolving, influenced by economic trends, technology, and changing consumer behaviors. Successful investors are those who can adapt to these changes and adjust their strategies accordingly. I've seen firsthand how properties that once thrived can become obsolete if they aren't updated to meet new market demands. Conversely, properties that have been overlooked can become valuable assets with the right vision and repositioning.

For example, I once owned a suburban office building that was struggling with high vacancy rates due to the shift toward urban workspaces and remote work. Instead of selling the property at a loss, I decided to repurpose it into a flexible workspace that catered to small businesses and startups, and we focused on governmental tenants which would commit to long term leases. We painted the exterior of the building, we upgraded the lobby, the elevators, the common areas and the landscaping. The transformation was a success, and the building quickly reached full occupancy.

The National Real Estate Investor reports that investors who can adapt to changing market conditions, such as repurposing underperforming properties, are more likely to achieve higher returns on investment. Being open to change and staying informed about market trends can provide a competitive edge in a rapidly shifting landscape.

Learning Continuously and Seeking Knowledge

Continuous learning is a vital part of success in commercial real estate. The industry is complex, with ever-changing regulations, financing structures, and market dynamics. To stay ahead, you need to keep expanding your knowledge and be open to new ideas. I make it a habit to attend real estate seminars, read industry publications, and seek out mentors who provide valuable insights. This commitment to learning helped me stay informed about the latest trends and best practices.

One of the most valuable lessons I learned was from a mortgage broker at a finance workshop. The presenter discussed creative financing strategies, including using seller financing. These techniques were new to me, but I decided to incorporate them into my investment strategy. As a result, I was able to close deals that I would have otherwise passed up due to lack of traditional financing.

Mentorship also plays a significant role in continuous learning. Throughout my career, I've sought out mentors who have more experience in certain areas of real estate. Their guidance not only helped me avoid costly mistakes but also provided me with different perspectives on approaching challenges and they were sources of strength during difficult times

The Building Owners and Managers Association (BOMA) highlights the importance of ongoing education for real estate professionals, noting that those who invest in their own development are better equipped to handle complex transactions and stay competitive in the industry.

Practicing Integrity and Building Trust

Integrity is the foundation of any successful career in real estate. Deals are often made based on trust, and your reputation is one of your most valuable assets. I've always made it a priority to act with honesty and transparency, even if it meant walking away from a deal that wasn't in my client's best interest.

In business everyone will occasionally encounter bad actors or bad partners. The key is to remain true to your principles and weather the storm. Their gossip will pass and your long-term history of doing the right thing will prevail over the long run.

I remember a situation where a partner stole money from our accounts. It was a sad time as we trusted him and his actions led to a big burden on the remaining team to clean up the mess and the partners to cover the loss.

However, that individual was out of the business within one year and the experience, although painful, resulted in much better controls and systems and made us a better team overall.

The Real Estate Marketing Association emphasizes that building trust through integrity not only fosters strong client relationships but also leads to long-term business success. Clients and partners appreciate transparency, and honesty even in the face of serious challenges and this can set you apart from competitors.

Leading by Example

As an investor, broker, or property manager, your actions set the tone for those around you. Leading by example means demonstrating the qualities you want to see in others, whether it's hard work, ethical behavior, or a commitment to excellence. I've always made it a point to be hands-on in my projects, from meeting with contractors and inspecting properties to working closely with my team to resolve issues. This approach not only motivates those I work with but also ensures that I have a deep understanding of my investments.

One of the most significant leadership moments in my career was when a major tenant in one of my office buildings experienced financial difficulties and struggled to keep up with rent payments. Instead of immediately taking legal action, I met with the tenant's management team and learned more about their situation. We worked out a modified payment plan that allowed them to stay in the space, while still protecting the property's cash flow. By taking a leadership role and showing flexibility, I was able to retain a good tenant, avoid legal costs, and maintain the building's occupancy.

I have always found a good settlement is better than any litigation. I have found that those who run to the courts are the ones with less character than those who will sit down and work through issues collaboratively.

According to research from the Urban Land Institute, leaders who actively engage with their projects and lead by example are more effective in managing teams, resolving conflicts, and achieving their investment goals. Being involved in your business at every level can give you a competitive edge and help build a strong, motivated team.

Setting a Vision for the Future

A clear vision is essential for guiding your team and your real estate investments. It provides direction, sets goals, and helps you stay focused on long-term objectives. When I first started in the industry, my vision was simple: to create innovative projects and build a diverse portfolio that generated passive income. Over time, my vision evolved to include revitalizing historic properties, pioneering sustainable development in Miami, and mentoring other investors.

I found that setting a vision not only helped me stay motivated but also attracted like-minded partners who shared my goals. For example, when I decided to focus on sustainable development, I connected with architects, contractors, and government officials who were passionate about green building practices. This network of professionals helped me achieve my goals more efficiently and opened doors to new opportunities.

The Real Estate Finance Journal recommends that investors regularly review and adjust their vision to account for changing market conditions and personal aspirations. A strong vision not only drives success but also provides a sense of purpose and fulfillment.

CHAPTER 10:

The Future of Commercial Real Estate—Embracing Innovation and New Opportunities

The commercial real estate industry is evolving rapidly, driven by technological innovations, shifts in consumer behavior, and a growing emphasis on sustainability. These changes present new challenges, but they also offer unprecedented opportunities for investors who are willing to adapt and embrace emerging trends. Throughout my career, I've learned that staying ahead of the curve isn't just about being aware of what's coming next; it's about actively seeking out new opportunities and being open to change.

In this chapter, I'll explore some of the key trends shaping the future of commercial real estate and discuss how to leverage them to stay competitive. These trends include the rise of smart building technologies, the importance of sustainability, the impact of flexible work arrangements, and the increasing use of data analytics. By understanding these developments and incorporating them into your investment strategy, you can better position yourself for long-term success.

The Rise of Smart Building Technologies

Smart building technologies are transforming the way commercial properties are managed and operated. These technologies, which include Internet of Things (IoT) sensors, automated lighting systems, and advanced HVAC controls, enable building owners and managers to monitor and optimize the performance of their properties in real time. The adoption of smart building systems can lead to significant cost savings by reducing energy consumption, improving operational efficiency, and enhancing tenant comfort.

I first encountered the potential of smart building technology while managing a large office complex that was struggling with high utility costs. We decided to implement a smart energy management system that included sensors to monitor lighting and temperature, as well as automated controls to adjust these settings based on occupancy and time of day. The result was a significant reduction in energy consumption and lower operating costs. Tenants also appreciated the enhanced comfort and control over their workspaces, which helped increase tenant retention.

According to the Building Owners and Managers Association (BOMA), properties equipped with smart building technology can achieve energy savings of up to 30%, while also increasing tenant satisfaction. As technology continues to evolve, the integration of artificial intelligence (AI) and machine learning will further enhance the ability of smart systems to predict maintenance needs, optimize resource use, and improve the overall tenant experience.

Embracing Sustainability and Green Building Practices

Sustainability has become a critical consideration in commercial real estate, with an increasing number of tenants, investors, and regulators demanding environmentally responsible buildings. Green building practices, such as using sustainable materials, incorporating energy-efficient systems, and pursuing certifications like LEED not only benefit the environment but also enhance a property's marketability and value.

One of the projects that stands out in my career was the development of Miami Green, the city's first LEED-certified Class A office building development. At the time, sustainable development was still a relatively new concept in the market, but I believed that the future of real estate would be shaped by environmental considerations. We developed the building next to Light rail, bus service and a green trolley system. In the building we used energy-efficient materials, installed a rooftop garden to help with insulation, designed HVAC with more fresh air coming into the building, and implemented water-saving fixtures throughout the building. The project was a success, attracting high-quality tenants who valued sustainable features and were willing to pay a premium for the space.

The U.S. Green Building Council reports that green buildings tend to have lower operating costs, higher occupancy rates, and increased property values compared to conventional buildings. As regulations around carbon emissions and energy efficiency continue to tighten, sustainable practices will be essential for meeting compliance and maintaining a competitive edge in the market.

Adapting to the Shift Toward Flexible Work Arrangements

The rise of remote work and flexible work arrangements has significantly impacted the commercial real estate landscape, especially in the office sector. As more companies adopt hybrid models that combine in-office and remote work, the demand for traditional office space has declined. However, this shift also presents opportunities for creative investors who are willing to rethink how office spaces are designed and utilized.

In response to changing tenant needs, I began to incorporate flexible leasing options and shared amenities into some of my office properties. For instance, I converted underutilized conference rooms into shared co-working spaces and added amenities like fitness centers, cafés, and outdoor seating areas. These changes made the properties more appealing to tenants who wanted a flexible, collaborative workspace. This strategy not only helped fill vacant space but also allowed for higher rent premiums due to the added value.

Research from the National Real Estate Investor indicates that demand for flexible office space, including co-working arrangements, is expected to grow by 21% annually over the next five years. Investors who adapt their properties to accommodate this trend will be better positioned to attract tenants and maintain high occupancy rates.

Leveraging Data Analytics for Smarter Decision-Making

Data analytics has become an indispensable tool in commercial real estate, enabling investors and property managers to make informed decisions based on real-time data and predictive insights. The use of data analytics allows for more accurate property valuations, better market forecasts, and improved tenant management. From analyzing demographic trends to tracking tenant behavior, data-driven insights can uncover opportunities that may not be immediately apparent through traditional methods.

I began integrating data analytics into my real estate strategy several years ago when I was considering expanding into new markets. Instead of relying solely on intuition and anecdotal information, I used demographic data, rental rate trends, and absorption rates to identify areas with strong growth potential. This approach helped me make more informed investment decisions and avoid markets that were oversaturated or on the decline.

According to the Real Estate Finance Journal, investors who leverage data analytics are better equipped to identify emerging trends, assess market risks, and maximize returns. By using data to guide your decision-making, you can gain a competitive edge and position your investments for long-term success.

The Growing Importance of Mixed-Use Developments

Mixed-use developments, which combine residential, commercial, and recreational spaces, have become increasingly popular as cities seek to create more walkable, integrated communities. These developments offer a variety of benefits, including increased foot traffic for retail tenants, higher occupancy rates, and enhanced property value. By combining different property types within a single project, mixed-use developments provide a hedge against market fluctuations in any one sector.

I became a strong advocate for mixed-use development after working on the first Major mixed-use building in Miami on Brickell Avenue. The development included retail space, office suites, residential units, and a condo hotel. The diverse mix of uses attracted a wide range of tenants and visitors, creating a dynamic environment that benefited the entire community. The project's success reinforced the idea that mixed-use properties could generate higher returns by catering to multiple needs within a single location.

The Urban Land Institute reports that mixed-use developments often command higher rental rates and property values compared to single-use properties due to their ability to attract diverse tenant groups. Investors who explore mixed-use opportunities can benefit from increased flexibility and resilience in their portfolios.

Integrating Technology to Enhance the Tenant Experience

The tenant experience is becoming a key differentiator in the commercial real estate market, with technology playing a central role in meeting tenant expectations. From mobile apps that facilitate seamless access to building services to virtual concierge platforms that offer amenities such as package delivery and maintenance requests, technology can significantly enhance the tenant experience.

I started incorporating tenant experience technology in some of my properties by providing tenants with access to a mobile app that allowed them to manage service requests, book shared amenities, and stay updated on building events. The app also offered an option for tenants to provide feedback, which helped me identify areas for improvement and make data-driven decisions to enhance tenant satisfaction.

A survey conducted by the Real Estate Marketing Association found that properties offering integrated technology solutions reported higher tenant retention rates and greater overall tenant satisfaction. As more tenants prioritize technology and convenience, integrating tenant-focused solutions will become increasingly important for property owners who want to stay competitive.

Preparing for the Impact of E-commerce on Industrial Real Estate

The rapid growth of e-commerce has dramatically changed the landscape of industrial real estate. As demand for online shopping continues to rise, so does the need for logistics and distribution facilities. Warehouses, fulfillment centers, and last-mile delivery hubs have become highly sought-after assets, especially in markets with strong transportation infrastructure.

I saw the impact of e-commerce firsthand when I worked on a team in an industrial and office park near Miami International Airport. The property was initially underutilized, but as e-commerce demand surged, the space became attractive to logistics companies looking for a well-positioned distribution hub. By upgrading the facility with enhanced loading docks, high-speed internet, and advanced security features, I was able to secure long-term leases with reputable tenants, resulting in a substantial increase in the property's value.

The National Association of Realtors reports that industrial properties catering to e-commerce companies have experienced rent growth that outpaces other commercial sectors. Investors who understand the unique requirements of e-commerce tenants and invest in properties that meet these needs can capitalize on the sector's growth.

The Role of Alternative Financing and Crowdfunding in Real Estate

The emergence of alternative financing options, such as real estate crowdfunding and online investment platforms, has democratized access to commercial real estate investments. These platforms allow individual investors to participate in projects that were previously only accessible to institutional investors. For developers and property owners, alternative financing provides a way to raise capital more quickly and efficiently.

I am currently exploring real estate crowdfunding to finance a multifamily development. By offering a portion of the equity to individual investors through a crowdfunding platform, I hope to raise the necessary funds without relying on traditional investors. The experience will hopefully not only provide me with a new way to access capital but also expand my network of investors who are interested in participating in future projects.

Research from the Real Estate Finance Journal indicates that crowdfunding and alternative financing can offer more flexible terms and lower financing costs compared to traditional loans. As these platforms continue to evolve, they will provide additional opportunities for both investors and developers to access the commercial real estate market.

Looking Forward: Staying Ahead of the Curve

The future of commercial real estate will be shaped by a combination of technological advancements, changing consumer preferences, and evolving market dynamics. To stay ahead of the curve, it's essential to continuously monitor these trends, invest in innovative solutions, and be prepared to adapt. Successful investors are those who don't just follow trends—they anticipate them and position themselves to capitalize on new opportunities.

One of the strategies I've adopted is setting aside a portion of my investment budget specifically for emerging trends, such as PropTech (property technology), sustainable development, and adaptive reuse. By dedicating resources to exploring these areas, I'm able to stay informed about new developments and remain agile in my approach.

The Urban Land Institute advises real estate professionals to prioritize innovation and embrace new technologies that enhance property performance and tenant experiences. This forward-thinking approach can lead to competitive advantages and drive long-term growth.

Taking Action and Planning for Your Next Steps

Commercial real estate is more than just a business—it's a journey filled with twists, turns, and immense possibilities for growth. This book aims to equip you with the tools, strategies, and mindset needed to navigate this industry successfully. However, the real value lies not just in the knowledge shared but in how you apply it. As we conclude, it's time to take these insights and put them into action. The journey ahead will challenge you, but with a clear vision, the right approach, and a commitment to learning, you can transform your aspirations into achievements.

Don't just read the book: TAKE ACTION Now!

Reflecting on the Path Taken

It's important to look back and recognize the steps that have brought you to this point. Reflection is more than simply assessing past experiences; it's about understanding how each moment has shaped you as an investor and a leader. The real estate industry is known for its unpredictability, and your career will likely be marked by both thrilling successes and daunting setbacks. What matters is how you learn from each situation and grow stronger.

In several periods of my career, I often felt like I was taking two steps forward and one step back. There were deals that fell apart at the last minute, unexpected maintenance costs that ate into profits, and legal issues that seemed impossible to navigate. But each challenge carried with it a valuable lesson. I learned the importance of meticulous due diligence, systems and checks and balances; gained a better understanding of local market dynamics and discovered how to negotiate more effectively.

One experience that comes to mind Involving a multi-family development. I had assembled a strong team and, but after purchasing the land the financing market dried up and we were stuck. At first, the situation felt overwhelming, and I questioned whether the project would ever be completed profitably. But as I worked through each obstacle—consulting with experts, listening to underwriters on what deals were getting financed, re-designing and re-zoning the property for more units and even leveraging the setback to secure additional equity from partners—it became apparent that the project was teaching me lessons I couldn't have learned in any other way.

By reflecting on these experiences, you not only recognize your growth but also build confidence in your ability to handle future challenges. Real estate is a business where resilience and a positive mindset can make all the difference.

Setting a Vision and Creating a Roadmap

Long-term success in commercial real estate begins with a clear vision. What do you want your career to look like five, ten, or even twenty years from now? Is your goal to build a large portfolio of commercial properties, develop iconic projects that reshape city skylines, or focus on creating sustainable, community-centered spaces? Your vision will be your guiding light, providing direction and motivation when you encounter tough times.

When I first began setting goals in real estate, I started with a simple objective: to acquire properties that generated enough income to fund future investments. As I achieved that initial goal, my vision expanded. I now set my sights on developing mixed-use projects, revitalizing historic buildings, and even venturing into different asset classes like industrial and medical office space. The key is to always have a roadmap that broke down the larger vision into smaller, achievable steps.

Creating a roadmap involves setting milestones that act as checkpoints on your journey. Each milestone represents a significant achievement—whether it's acquiring your first property, completing a renovation project, or reaching a certain cash flow threshold. The advantage of having milestones is that they provide a sense of progress, which is crucial for maintaining motivation over the long term. It's important to celebrate these wins, even the small ones, because they contribute to building the momentum needed for larger accomplishments.

In our firm, we celebrate progress and not just the result or profitability which might be measured five or ten years later.

While having a plan is essential, flexibility is equally important. The roadmap you create today may need to be adjusted as market conditions evolve or new opportunities arise. For example, there were times in my career when a project required pivoting midway—whether due to changes in local regulations or shifts in tenant demand. In these situations, being adaptable was crucial. Rather than abandoning the original goal, I would find new ways to reach it, such as repositioning a property for a different use or seeking out alternative financing solutions.

Learning Through Action and Adaptation

The real estate industry is not a static environment. It's a dynamic space where markets shift, technologies evolve, and new opportunities continuously emerge. The best way to stay ahead is through continuous action and adaptation. It's often said that the best way to learn is by doing, and in real estate, this couldn't be truer. Every deal you engage in, every negotiation you undertake, and every tenant relationship you manage will teach you invaluable lessons that you can't get from books alone.

For example, when I first expanded into retail properties, I had to navigate a completely different set of challenges than I was familiar with in office spaces. Retail involved understanding foot traffic patterns, consumer behavior, and even the intricacies of lease structures for different types of tenants. I made some mistakes along the way, such as overestimating demand in certain areas, which resulted in vacancies that took longer than expected to fill. However, by closely analyzing what went wrong and adjusting my approach—such as diversifying the tenant mix and offering flexible lease terms—I eventually found a formula that worked.

Adaptation is not about abandoning your initial strategy at the first sign of trouble; it's about being willing to make the necessary adjustments to improve outcomes. The real estate market is influenced by countless factors, from economic cycles to technological advancements and shifting consumer preferences. The ability to pivot your approach when faced with these changes is what will set you apart as an investor.

The Power of Relationships and Community

As much as commercial real estate is a business of properties and numbers, it is also a business of people. Relationships form the backbone of your success. The connections you build with partners, contractors, tenants, and even competitors can open doors to new opportunities and help you navigate challenges. Throughout my career, I've seen deals come together not just because of financial considerations but because of the trust and rapport I had established with key players in the industry.

Networking is not just about collecting business cards or adding connections on social media. It's about building meaningful relationships where both parties see value in the exchange. Whether you're offering advice, sharing industry insights, or simply providing a listening ear, your efforts to help others will eventually come back to you in unexpected ways. Aside from business, consider how your real estate activities can contribute positively to the community. Participating in local events, supporting charitable initiatives, or even volunteering your expertise to local causes can enhance your reputation and open more opportunities.

Anticipating Future Changes and Staying Ahead

The commercial real estate landscape is undergoing rapid transformation. With the rise of new technologies, changing consumer behaviors, and evolving regulatory frameworks, the industry today looks very different from what it was even a decade ago. Staying ahead of these changes requires not just awareness but a proactive approach to integrating new ideas and practices.

Consider the growing importance of sustainability. Today, tenants and investors are increasingly prioritizing eco-friendly buildings with features such as energy-efficient lighting, green roofs, and sustainable materials. Early in my career, I began incorporating these elements into my projects, not only to attract quality tenants but also to future-proof my investments against tightening environmental regulations. That forward-thinking approach paid off when certain jurisdictions began offering tax incentives for green building practices thereby giving my properties a competitive advantage.

Similarly, technology is revolutionizing how properties are managed and marketed. Smart building systems, data analytics, and even AI-driven tenant management platforms are transforming the industry. Investors who embrace these innovations can significantly reduce operational costs, improve tenant satisfaction, and gain insights that drive better decision-making. Staying ahead of technological trends requires a willingness to experiment and the courage to invest in new systems that may seem unproven at first.

But being future-focused doesn't mean chasing every new trend. It involves carefully assessing which innovations align with your goals and market conditions. The key is to strike a balance between embracing change and sticking to the proven principles that have guided you thus far.

Leaving a Lasting Legacy

When I think about what truly defines success in commercial real estate, it goes beyond financial returns, or the number of properties owned. It's about the legacy you leave behind—the impact you make on the communities you touch, the lives you improve, and the places you help transform. Every building tells a story, and as a developer, investor, or property manager, you have the opportunity to shape that narrative.

Some of the most rewarding projects I've worked on involved not just developing profitable properties but revitalizing communities.

As you continue your journey, think about the legacy you want to leave behind. Real estate gives you the power to shape cities and communities in ways that only a few other professions can. Whether it's through sustainable development, mentoring young professionals, or simply treating tenants and partners with respect, your actions will define your legacy.

A Final Call to Action

The principles and strategies shared in this book are designed to serve as a foundation for your real estate journey. However, no amount of reading can replace the need for action. Take what you've learned, set your goals, and start implementing the strategies that resonate most with your vision. Real estate is a long-term game, and there will be challenges along the way. But each step you take, each deal you pursue, and each lesson you learn will bring you closer to your aspirations.

Remember that success is not a destination but a continuous process of growth, adaptation, and resilience. As you navigate the world of commercial real estate, stay committed to your vision, keep learning, and never be afraid to take calculated risks. The path ahead is yours to shape—go out and make your mark.

Sources:

1. National Association of Realtors.
2. Deloitte. "Commercial Real Estate Outlook 2023."
3. PwC Real Estate 2023 Trends
4. Property Metrics. "Understanding Debt Service Coverage Ratio in Commercial Real Estate."
5. Commercial Real Estate Financing Guide by Investopedia.
6. National Association of Real Estate Investment Trusts (NAREIT).
7. Building Owners and Managers Association (BOMA).
8. CBRE. "Impact of Green Building Features on Property Value and Tenant Satisfaction."
9. U.S. Green Building Council. "The Value of LEED Certification for Commercial Properties."
10. Urban Land Institute. "The Importance of Data and Technology in Commercial Real Estate."
11. Real Estate Finance Journal.
12. National Real Estate Investor.
13. HubSpot. "The Value of Video Content in Digital Marketing."
14. Real Estate Marketing Association.
15. Institute of Real Estate Management (IREM).
16. U.S. Green Building Council.

www.ingramcontent.com/pod-product-compliance
Lightning Source LLC
Chambersburg PA
CBHW071038240526
45469CB00006BD/2246